REF
PR
9199.3
.B3418
S57
1998

HWLCLT

Chicago Public Library

D1245553

LITERATURE AND LANGUAGE DIVISION
LITERATURE INFORMATION CENTER
CHICAGO PUBLIC LIBRARY
400 SOUTH STATE STREET
CHICAGO, ILLINOIS 60605

Chicago Public Library

REFERENCE

Form 178 rev. 1-94

# sistahs

## maxine bailey & sharon m. lewis

Playwrights Canada Press
Toronto • Canada

*Sistahs* © maxine bailey and sharon m. lewis, 1994

**Playwrights Canada Press** is the publishing imprint of:
*Playwrights Union of Canada*
*54 Wolseley Street, 2nd floor, Toronto, Ontario, M5T 1A5*
*Tel (416) 703-0201; Fax (416) 703-0059*
*E-mail: cdplays@interlog.com; Internet: www.puc.ca*

**CAUTION:** This play is fully protected under the copyright laws of Canada and all other countries of The Copyright Union, and is subject to royalty. Changes to the script are expressly forbidden without the prior written permission of the author. Rights to produce, film, or record, in whole or in part, in any medium or any language, by any group, amateur or professional, are retained by the author. Those interested are requested to apply for all production rights to: *Playwrights Union of Canada.*

No part of this book, covered by the copyright hereon, may be reproduced or used in any form or by any means—graphic, electronic or mechanical—without the prior written permission of the publisher except for excerpts in a review. Any request for photocopying, recording, taping or information storage and retrieval systems of any part of this book shall be directed to: *The Canadian Copyright Licensing Agency*
*6 Adelaide Street East, Suite 900, Toronto, Ontario, M5C 1H6*
*Tel (416) 868-1620; Fax (416) 868-1621*

U.S. sales and distribution: *Theatre Communications Group, 355 Lexington Avenue, New York, NY, 10077-0217, USA.*

**Playwrights Canada Press** operates with the generous assistance of The Canada Council for the Arts—Writing and Publishing Section, and the Ontario Arts Council—Literature Office.

**Canadian Cataloguing in Publication Data**

Lewis, Sharon, 1965-
    Sistahs

A play
ISBN 0-88754-553-X

I Bailey, Maxine, 1959-    II. Title.

PS8573.E9875S57  1998       C812'.54       C98-930154-0
PR9199.3.L474S57  1998

Cover art: Paul Gladden. Photo of maxine bailey: Michael Chambers. Photo of sharon m. lewis: Joan Lauren

First Edition: November 1998
Printed and bound in Winnipeg, Manitoba: Hignell Printing

# Preface

An extraordinary play. A succulent read. Poignant, passionate, tender, moving, and funny as all hell. maxine bailey and sharon m. lewis have created a host of wonderful characters that seem to jump right off the page. The beautifully complex form reflects the depth and breadth of each character's humanity. A Dutch pot is the psycho-physical and metaphorical container for an epicurian balm. They are alchemists, and the alchemists' gold is a luxurious Trinidadian broth, a prescription, a therapy born of death's imminence. A cauldron steams, bubbles, and simmers the medicine: part stew, part soup, part wholistic remedy to soothe the swelling tumour or approaching grief. I am told that there was a time when cooking and pharmacology were the same thing. There is a strong suggestion that they have once again been reunited within these pages. This is a riveting and beautifully written story: rich in love; facing death; set in the heart of living.

There is a naissant groundswell of theatre writing by people of African descent and people of colour in Canada. Across the board, across the country: Andrei Alexis, George Elliott Clarke, Andrew Moodie, Diana Braithwaite, Ahdri Zhina Mandiela, Lorena Gayle, Michael Miller, Marlene Norbese Phillip, Richardo Keenes-Douglas, Joanne John, David Ohdiambo, to name but a few. Their plays reflect a multiplicity of dreams, desires, cultures, experiences, preferences, and ancestry. With *Sistahs*, maxine bailey and sharon m. lewis proudly add their names to a substantial and ever growing roster of AfriCanadian playwrights and playwrights of colour.

Djanet Sears

RO170865138

LITERATURE AND LANGUAGE DIVISION
LITERATURE INFORMATION CENTER
CHICAGO PUBLIC LIBRARY
400 SOUTH STATE STREET
CHICAGO, ILLINOIS 60605

# Playwrights' and Director's Notes

the play *sistahs* may have gone through a different process than other plays, since there were two women writing our stories and melding/ merging them together.

the process that we developed came about after many false starts and laughter. we agreed on a basic story. we agreed on the characters. the two biggies!

the toronto theatre scene was extremely supportive in terms of funding, and we were able to apply for funding for two workshops, one public, and our final professional production of the same play. during the direction of the public workshop, sharon was faced with the dilemma of having huge chunks of time when not all the characters on stage were involved with the primary scene. so, she had them echo their emotional state through movement and sound, which maxine and sharon incorporated into the final script. the second workshop was a closed writers' workshop with a cast available to the playwrights. by the end of the second workshop, we added sandra's lectures, and integrated them with movement. we took her lectures and integrated them with the "ancestral time." consequently, ancestral time became connected to the voices of the older generation of the characters.

"lecture mode" came out of our need to show sandra's life, existence, and her personal history before her illness. the deterioration that takes place in sandra's personal health, parallels the passage of slavery to its present day manifestations. in the beginning the lectures are quite clear, as sandra herself is able to separate her own life from the historical life she's talking about. but later on, her illness forces a convergence of these two existences.

"real time" is self-explanatory. it is. but as with our own lives, there are overlaps in the voices that guide us.

rhythm is essential to this piece. the convergence of voices and the backdrop of the ancestral movements and sounds are as important to this piece as the dialogue.

# Acknowledgements

*sistahs* is a work of love that was born from a sisterhood sharon lewis felt with her co-writer maxine bailey; from the love of cooking and family she got from her father, mother, and many aunts, uncles, and cousins; and from her many sistahs, including melanie nicholls-king, debbie tungatt, dawn stephenson, rachael crawford, mo jen, and all the participants that brought the drama its life.

the process of creating *sistahs* was literally like soup. you start off with a taste for something, you put it in the pot, it still needs some livening up, you add some more spice, the end result being something you'd never imagined and, sadly, are not able to recreate. but damn, it tastes good. here's a list of the key ingredients for the soup that took two years to simmer. if your name isn't here, it's not a slight. go directly to the last acknowledgment. thanks to all who supported us:

ahdri zhina mandiela, anika and akosa holder, anji, april bailey, arthi, bryan james, cahoots theatre, cameron bailey, the canada council explorations program, *canadian theatre review*, carol anderson, carol camper, catherine bruhier, christine buckell, company of sirens, cynthia grant, dahlia ashley ho sue, dawn stephenson, de poonani posse, the department of canadian heritage, diana sookdeo, diane roberts, dirk mclean, djanet sears, *fuse magazine*, gwen bartleman, jennifer jenkins, joan pierre, jon kaplan, karen augustine, kate lushington, kathleen lewis, kathleen daniels, kay valley, ken montague, kirk king, kim roberts, kimberly huie, lennox and carol king, lisa richardson, luciene bailey, lynda hill, maureen anatole, marilyn gomes, melanie nicholls-king, michael miller, nightwood theatre, the ontario arts council, patrice behn, rachel giese, rachel kalpana james, rene chan, roger grubb, sally han, sandi ross, shakura s'aida, shaun ray boyd, sky gilbert, sonia dhillon, stanley lewis, stephanie samuels, tabby johnson, tarragon theatre, the betty ford, the performing artists' lodge, the toronto arts council, tricia williams, vashti, young people's theatre, and sherece taffe. to all the folks who supported us by giving cash and coming to our many fundraising events, who came to the play, donated time, energy, or merchandise, A HUGE BIG-UP TO YOU!

*to my daughter april*
*may you find what you're looking for*
*and to a friend who believed*
*and wouldn't let me stop writing*

maxine bailey


*to stanley telpher lewis, my father*
*who in his death made me understand*
*the "life" of sistahs*

sharon m. lewis

maxine bailey was born in England, manages to reside in Toronto, yet yearns to be a resident of Barbados. She writes, directs, and produces theatre in Toronto, in that order. Sometimes, rarely, and constantly. She works at being an attentive mother, sistah, daughter, and friend to all the wonderful folks in her life.

sharon mareeka lewis is a callaloo mix of Trinidadian and Jamaican heritage. She is a professional actor, published writer, producer, and director who was born and raised in Toronto, Canada. sharon graduated from the University of Toronto with an honours degree in political science. She combined her political activism with her penchant for drama and worked in political theatre. She then co-founded "Sugar 'n' Spice," a production company devoted to producing works by and for women of colour, and has continued her career in the entertainment field in Los Angeles.

# Production History

*Sistahs* was first produced in Toronto, Canada, by Sugar 'n' Spice Productions at the Poor Alex Theatre, in October 1994.

| | |
|---|---|
| maxine bailey | Playwright/Producer/Costume Designer |
| sharon m. lewis | Playwright/Director |
| Bryan James | Set Designer |
| Christine Buckell | Lighting and Sound Designer |
| Diana Sookdeo | Stage Manager |
| Sonia Dhillon | Assistant Stage Manager |
| Fleurette S. Fernando | Choreographer |

| | |
|---|---|
| SANDRA | Melanie Nicholls-King * |
| DEHLIA | Lisa Richardson |
| ASSATA | Carol Anderson |
| REA | Kim Roberts |
| CERISE | Shakura S'Aida |

* Best Actress Dora Award nomination, 1994

# Glossary

*Ancestral time*:  slow, repetitive movements

*Lecture mode*:  refers to Sandra

*Real time*:  happening in the present

# The Sistahs

SANDRA:  mid-thirties, history professor

DEHLIA:  thirties, Sandra's lover, coordinator of a women's centre

ASSATA:  sixteen years old, Sandra's daughter, a student

REA:  early thirties, Sandra's half-sister, government bureaucrat

CERISE:  thirties, family friend, filmmaker

# The Setting

A warm, bright, large apartment. The kitchen is centre stage, signified by a huge, old, wooden kitchen table with five wooden stools at varying heights. Worn shelving, with five huge ceramic bowls and five large wooden spoons resting inside the bowls, forms the backdrop. A large stand/stove for the soup. The living room is signified by an overstuffed loveseat and a beatbox. Other rooms/spaces are representational.

## Dessert                                    Prologue

| | |
|---|---|
| **SANDRA** | Then came the sullen acceptance that their fate was to serve, be born, work, and die under threat...? |

        ASSATA *steps out of the shadows and joins her mother.*

| | |
|---|---|
| **ASSATA** | Kill the gravillicious... cells. |

        DEHLIA *joins* SANDRA *and* ASSATA.

| | |
|---|---|
| **DEHLIA** | You never see cells on their own. |

        CERISE *joins* SANDRA, DEHLIA, *and* ASSATA.

| | |
|---|---|
| **CERISE** | Provide? Yeah, I was busy providing... a martyr of a mother. |
| **SANDRA** | I carry my story in my womb. Most women do, but not all. How many of you are...? |

        REA *joins* SANDRA, DEHLIA, ASSATA, *and* CERISE.

| | |
|---|---|
| **REA** | They know no boundaries. |
| **CERISE** | Even a mother's womb is not a safe home for her child. |
| **ASSATA** | *(giggling)* In one soup is the taste of all our mothers. |
| **SANDRA** | The end... signaled? |

        *Lights down.*

# The Preparation                    Scene One

> *Early morning.* SANDRA *has her head in the oven, cleaning it out.*

**SANDRA** Assata, *(pause)* Assata, ASSATTTTA!!

> ASSATA *enters the kitchen, sleepily.*

**ASSATA** I'm here, you don't have to yell.

> ASSATA *is not paying attention, has found her walkwoman, and is rapping along.*

**SANDRA** We have people coming over you can't help clean up the house this one time. *(sucks her teeth)* I've been trying to wake you since seven o'clock.

**ASSATA** I can't hear you, what areya saying?

> SANDRA *comes out of the oven.*

**SANDRA** How are you ever going to learn—

> *She notices the walkwoman, takes it off.*

**ASSATA** What?

> ASSATA *slouches at the table.*

**SANDRA** *(pointing to walkwoman)* This is why I yell.

**ASSATA** You don't have to yell, I know what you were saying.

**SANDRA** How are you ever going to learn how to keep house if—

ASSATA    Mom, I'm shocked! You a *feminist* mother, *forcing* your daughter to learn how to keep house.

SANDRA    Very funny, you know very well you don't do a damn thing around this house.

        SANDRA *goes back to cleaning/preparing.*

ASSATA    I dusted.

        ASSATA *starts tinkering with her walkwoman.*

SANDRA    When?!

ASSATA    Last week. *(pause)* What are Auntie Rea and them bringing? I hope it's not that slimy, potatoey thing.

SANDRA    Who is them?

ASSATA    Cerise.

SANDRA    What happen to *Auntie* Cerise?

ASSATA    Cerise told me I could call her by her first name.

SANDRA    Not in my house.

ASSATA    I thought you said this is *our* house.

SANDRA    Go clean up the bathroom.

ASSATA    Done. Will me cleaning house make you better?

SANDRA    Assata, we've been through this.

ASSATA    I just wanna know how making a soup is going to make you better?

SANDRA    I never said it would make me bettah.

ASSATA    Well, why do it?

SANDRA    It can't hurt.

ASSATA       Well I don't know, it depends on who's doing the cooking.

SANDRA       Assata I am tir—

ASSATA       Well maybe you wouldn't be so tired if you would go back to the doctor and get that stupid cis-carb playtane.

SANDRA       Sounds like plantain. Carb—platin.

ASSATA       Why did you invite Auntie Rea, you don't even like her?

SANDRA       Time for things to change.

ASSATA       Obviously.

SANDRA       I told you before Assata it's time for me to make peace it's time for you too.

ASSATA       I don't have a problem with Auntie Re—

SANDRA       I mean peace with me, Assata.

---

# The Preparation       Scene Two

      DEHLIA *enters kitchen from living room with a bag of groceries, kisses* SANDRA, *and starts to unpack.*

DEHLIA       Girl, Kensington market was packed I've never seen it like that.

SANDRA       I love it when it's packed, it reminds me of back home.

DEHLIA       Back home again?

| | |
|---|---|
| **SANDRA** | Yeah Dee-Dee. |
| **ASSATA** | *(to* DEHLIA*)* Yeah Goo-Goo. |
| **DEHLIA** | *(back to* ASSATA*)* Yeah Ass-Yass. |
| | DEHLIA *throws a small bag of mangoes to* ASSATA. |
| **DEHLIA** | These are yours. Catch. |
| | ASSATA *catches them, does some stylish moves.* |
| **ASSATA** | Stylin'! |
| **DEHLIA** | *(to* ASSATA*)* Careful with those mangoes, Nicey's told me they are fresh off the boat from Jamaica. |
| **ASSATA** | *(looks at the mangoes)* Oh yeah, how come the sticker says "Made in Mexico." |
| **DEHLIA** | What! |
| **ASSATA** | Foolie! |
| **SANDRA** | *(to* ASSATA*)* I nevah hear about mango in soup. |
| **DEHLIA** | I got plantain. |
| **SANDRA** | I nevah hear 'bout plantain in soup. |
| **ASSATA** | I like my plantain fried. |
| **SANDRA** | Well then you better learn how to fry it. |
| | DEHLIA *throws* ASSATA *the plantain.* |
| **DEHLIA** | In Jamaica, we have gungo pea soup, red pea soup, cowfoot soup.... What kind of soup is "every body bring something soup"? |

| | |
|---|---|
| **SANDRA** | It's Wes' Indian. *(gets up, gets the mop and pail ready, and starts mopping the kitchen floor)* What would you know about cooking? You had Molly. |
| **DEHLIA** | Esta, how many times I haf to tell you the 'ooman's name is Esta! |
| **SANDRA** | *(pushing the mop)* Look Esta here now. |
| **DEHLIA** | *(eyeing SANDRA as she's bent over)* Well you don't look like Esta from behind. |
| **ASSATA** | That's because Mom has no behind. |
| **SANDRA** | *(to ASSATA)* You must be mixing me up with your Auntie Rea. |
| | DEHLIA *unpacks the sugar and throws it to* ASSATA. |
| **DEHLIA** | Always put a little brown sugar at the bottom of the pot. |
| **SANDRA** | Only if it's a Dutch pot. |
| **DEHLIA** | Where we come from, its called a dutchie. |
| **SANDRA** | Yeah, well where I come from, we know how to call things proper, not like you *small* island people. |
| **DEHLIA** | Whoevah hear of Trinidad, is Jamaica everyone know about, right Assata? |
| | DEHLIA *starts humming Rita Marley's "Pass the Dutchie," and* ASSATA *starts singing.* |
| **ASSATA** | "Pass the dutchie pun the lef hand side, me say pass the dutchie pun the lef hand side it go burn." |
| **SANDRA** | *(laughing to DEHLIA and ASSATA)* Well I see you all do know something about cooking? |

| | |
|---|---|
| **DEHLIA** | About proper Jamaican cooking. *(pause)* It's that Trini food we caan deal with. |
| **SANDRA** | Yeah well you seem to enjoy Trini dining. |

> SANDRA *kisses* DEHLIA.

| | |
|---|---|
| **ASSATA** | Mom... Natalie wants me to come over... after dinner |
| **SANDRA** | What do you think? |
| **ASSATA** | I was just asking. I've been inside helping you and I haven't seen Natalie *all* day. |
| **SANDRA** | You've been on the phone to her at least three different times today and its only ten o'clock. |
| **ASSATA** | Its not the same. |
| **SANDRA** | I'm not going to get into this, if you want to go, ask *your* Dehlia. |
| **ASSATA** | *(interjects)* BUT—! |
| **SANDRA** | NO. *(pause)* You satisfied now. *(mutters under her breath, as she gets the mop and pail and moves towards the bathroom)* Bathroom not done right, I might as well do it. |

> *Ancestral time.* SANDRA *moves in a circular mopping motion towards the space that represents the bathroom. She continues this circular motion, the movement becomes a larger dance movement, until the rhythm and movement brings her to the living room.*

## The Preparation                    Scene Three

ASSATA *and* DEHLIA *in the kitchen.*

**DEHLIA**      So wha' happen? You said you did the bathroom.

**ASSATA**      I did.

SANDRA *in the living room.*

**SANDRA**      She wants to help?! I'm the one mopping. NO, all she wanna to do is stand up and ask me question, why I don't take the treatment, why I don't see this and that doctor? When I'm not here, then she goes and runs street.

SANDRA *leans tiredly on the mop*

**DEHLIA**      Now *I* know you did the bathroom, *you* know you did the bathroom. Is your mother going to go and find the bathroom done her way?

**ASSATA**      Well....

**DEHLIA**      It's a big day.

**ASSATA**      I know.

**DEHLIA**      It's an important day.

**SANDRA**      She don't see a doctor standing up in front of her?

**ASSATA**      I knooow!

**SANDRA**      She thinks she knows everything.

**ASSATA**      I know it's an important day.

**DEHLIA**   Now I know you know, but do you know that I know, that you know.

**ASSATA**   Yeah, I know that you know that I know that you know.

**DEHLIA/
ASSATA**   *(simultaneously)* You know! *(laugh)* Boom.

*Pause.*

**DEHLIA**   She *doesn't* know that you know.

> DEHLIA *and* ASSATA *place the plantain, mangoes, and sugar on the table. Ancestral time. They continue putting away groceries in a repetitive motion that complements each other until Scene Four. As* SANDRA *continues talking, her movements take her back to the kitchen.*

**SANDRA**   She doesn't know I struggle everyday in this country. Sleet, snowstorms, blizzards, freezing rain, *(sucks her teeth)* nearly fall down on the ice carrying the child. Why can't she hear? I tried their way, this is for me.

**DEHLIA**   *(yelling from the kitchen)* Sandy you alright, you need some help?

**SANDRA**   NO. *(sighs quietly)* Yes.

> SANDRA *slowly puts the mop and pail in the bathroom and then moves into the kitchen. Lights down and spotlight up on* SANDRA *as she begins her lecture.*

How many of you are African? In the beginning there was confusion, battle, and disbelief that their own people had turned against them. Something had come into their life unwanted. First sign: states could not carry out their normal functions. Greetings. This is HIS 101. I'm professor Sandra Grange-Mosaku. For the next eight months we are going to be rethinking

World History. That's right not Third World, not
Emerging World, but the part of the world that's been
around, three trillion plus times and that's not
including eclipses.

> *Spot comes down. SANDRA returns to her
> original position, starts washing the Dutch pot,
> drying it. She puts sugar in the pot.*

A halfa handful of sugar at the bottom of the Dutch
pot, warm it until it dissolves. *(she fills pot with
cold water and puts it on the stove to boil)* If the soup
is for plenty people, add more water. (*DEHLIA and*
ASSATA *help* SANDRA *add more water for the
soup)* If you have a cold add some cayenne pepper. If
you have a fever make the broth light and add lots of
garlic. If you have—

> CERISE *yells from offstage.*

**CERISE**      If you have what?


# Peeling, Chopping, Cutting          Scene Four


> CERISE *yells from offstage.*

**CERISE**      If we have to have soup, put in lots of those
                dumplings.

> CERISE *enters the apartment, dumps her
> groceries in the living room, and continues into
> the kitchen.*

**SANDRA**      *(yelling to* CERISE) Cerise, what do you know about
                dumpling? You were born here.

> CERISE *enters kitchen, gives* SANDRA *a hug.*
> SANDRA *then moves away from the pot*
> *towards table, where fresh herbs await.*

**ASSATA**        Cerise!

**SANDRA**        Its Auntie Ce—

**CERISE**        Hey Assata, Dehlia.

**DEHLIA**        Only you could wear something like dat and get away
             with it.

**CERISE**        Honey close your mouth, I know I look good.

> SANDRA *starts to chop fresh herbs, such as*
> *thyme.*

**SANDRA**        But do you taste good?

**CERISE**        As fresh as that thyme you're chopping.

**DEHLIA**        Auntie Dotilda made dumplings once, but they never
             turn out like Esta's.

> *Pause.* SANDRA *knows it just another*
> *Dehlia-ism*

**SANDRA**        Rea and I are making them today.

**DEHLIA**        Rea is going to get her hands dirty?

**SANDRA**        You know she makes dumplings.

**CERISE**        Good. As long as she makes me those long, long...

**ASSATA**        ...long...

**SANDRA**        ...dumplings.

**CERISE**        Assata come help me bring in my groceries.

SANDRA          Groceries? I thought you were only bringing sweet
                potato.

CERISE          I brought potato, I'm sweet enough.

                *CERISE exits to living room. DEHLIA gets up
                and helps SANDRA chop the thyme. ASSATA
                picks up her walkwoman and mangoes, then
                follows CERISE to the living room. She hides
                the mangoes by the already hidden bowl, knife,
                and spices.*

# Peeling, Chopping, Cutting          Scene Five

                *DEHLIA and SANDRA in the kitchen, chopping
                the thyme.*

SANDRA          So what are you putting in the soup?

CERISE          So what are you doing over there?

                *ASSATA is hiding mangoes in the living room.
                CERISE gets her groceries.*

DEHLIA          I told you the plantain.

ASSATA          Never you mind.

                *ASSATA pulls out the recipe for "Mango
                Chow" and starts reading it.*

DEHLIA          But you've said you don't like plantain in soup so
                I'll—

SANDRA          No Dehlia, I told you to put in what you want to.
                Just add lots of...

CERISE          It's my job to mind.

> CERISE *moves towards* ASSATA *and starts reading over* ASSATA's *shoulder.*

**SANDRA**    ...pepper.

> CERISE *and* ASSATA *read the recipe out loud together once. Ancestral time. They quietly repeat it until* SANDRA's *lecture.*

**CERISE/**
**ASSATA**    Mango Chow:
green Julie mangoes
washed, peeled, and sliced in thin strips
add pipe water
add sea salt
vinegar
fresh lime
black pepper
and of course pepper sauce to taste
let sit
cover with a towel to keep the *(mumble)* away

**DEHLIA**    But if everyone puts in what they want how is it going to taste?

**SANDRA**    Just do it with love.

**DEHLIA**    I've got plenty of that.

> *She squeezes* SANDRA's *bum.* SANDRA *hands her the plantain to peel and chop.*

**SANDRA**    Good because the soup is for plenty people.

**DEHLIA**    It's only five of us.

**SANDRA**    That's enough.

> SANDRA *has a small, sharp pain.*

| | |
|---|---|
| **DEHLIA** | Why are you breaking your back to make the soup in this way*? (sits* SANDRA *down to massage and wrap her head)* How come you don't let me wrap your head anymore? |
| **SANDRA** | Not enough time. |
| **DEHLIA** | I thought you were going to make time. |
| **SANDRA** | If I could *make* time I wouldn't have to make this soup. |
| **DEHLIA** | Let me help you. |
| **SANDRA** | Make the soup? |
| **DEHLIA** | Make time. |
| **SANDRA** | C'mon we have to get the soup started. |
| **DEHLIA** | We're making the time. |

> DEHLIA *continues to massage and wrap* SANDRA*'s head.* SANDRA *gets up, spotlight comes up, and she moves into lecture mode.* DEHLIA *continues massaging motion, ancestral time.*

| | |
|---|---|
| **SANDRA** | Slavery does not develop on healthy sites. The cells must be stressed.... |

> *As* CERISE *and* ASSATA *are flipping through the recipe, words pop out.*

| | |
|---|---|
| **CERISE/ ASSATA** | Add sea salt... |
| **SANDRA** | Slavery based on race is the only kind of slavery that crossed geographical/national/political state boundaries.... |
| **CERISE/ ASSATA** | ...let sit... |

**SANDRA**    The second stage....

**CERISE/
ASSATA**    ...washed, peeled, and sliced...

**SANDRA**    Slavery was governed outside of the bodies that
produced the slaves. Okay, the middle passage. How
many of you can give me a definition of what that
was...?

**CERISE/
ASSATA**    ...cover with a towel to keep the *(mumble)* away.

**SANDRA**    Too early huh?

> *Ancestral time. Spotlight comes down and
> SANDRA returns to her original position in the
> chair, with DEHLIA massaging her head.*

# Peeling, Chopping, Cutting        Scene Six

> *ASSATA and CERISE finish looking at the
> Mango Chow recipe.*

**CERISE**    Does this go in the soup?

**ASSATA**    No.

**CERISE**    Green mango?

**ASSATA**    My granma told me this was Mom's favourite,
especially when she was pregnant.

**CERISE**    Yeah, trying to score brownie points.

**ASSATA**    It fits the criteria.

**CERISE**    All natural?

| | |
|---|---|
| **ASSATA** | Check. Mangoes fresh from Jamaica. |
| **CERISE** | Cultural relevance? |
| **ASSATA** | Strictly a Trinidadian recipe. |
| **CERISE** | Cheap too. |

> *Knock at the door.* CERISE *goes to open the door.* REA *enters.*

| | |
|---|---|
| **REA** | Oh hello Cerise, I didn't know everybody was here already. |
| **CERISE** | If everybody means me, I guess we're all here. |
| **REA** | Hello Assata. |
| **ASSATA** | *(loud and formally)* Hello, Auntie Rea. |

> *She kisses* REA *on the cheek, with a quick hug.* REA *puts the bags down.*

| | |
|---|---|
| **REA** | I haven't seen you since Christmas. You've grown. |
| **ASSATA** | I know it happens. |

> *She gestures to* ASSATA*'s afro.*

| | |
|---|---|
| **REA** | What's that? Afro? That's coming back now? |
| **CERISE** | Well in my time we called it a 'fro. Girl, I had me one to die for. Just like Angela Davis.... I was so upset when I found out it was a wig. |
| **ASSATA** | She has dreads. |

**CERISE**  In my time she had a 'fro. I got up two hours before school started to get the sleep dents out of my hair to have a perfectly rounded 'fro. This guy, what's his name... would just torture me. He'd mess it up with his fingers. He pushed me too far one time. I chased him with my afro pick.... I had me one of those metal ones.

> CERISE *play-stabs* ASSATA. ASSATA *blocks it.*

**ASSATA**  You don't look the type to be roughing people up.

**CERISE**  Baby, when it comes to black womens' hair, you know we don't mess. Do you let people touch up your hair?

**ASSATA**  Uh-uh. No way.

**CERISE**  I didn't think so.

**CERISE/ ASSATA**  *(in unison)* Hmhmmh!

> CERISE, REA, *and* ASSATA *laugh.*

**REA**  In school, PSYCH 101, I sat in front of Jack Becking. I kept feeling this tapping, and I'd turn around and Jack would be smiling, and I'd smile back. He was kind of cute too. Walking out of class, I heard these giggles, and when I turned around, I felt something on my neck. I ran my hand through my hair and ping... ping, two, three, about ten pencils fell out of my hair.

> REA *is laughing.* CERISE *and* ASSATA *are quiet.*

**ASSATA**  But Auntie Rea, your hair's so straight now.

| | |
|---|---|
| **REA** | Well, your mom had an afro, and I had to have one too. Before I left Trinidad, Sandra helped me fluff it up, and work with my natural curl. She loved it when I followed her style. |
| **CERISE** | So how'd it get so straight? |
| **REA** | I'm not fighting it. |
| **CERISE/REA/ ASSATA** | *(in unison)* Hmmmhmmmh. |

> SANDRA *enters living room.* DEHLIA *takes out her jigsaw puzzle on a tray and puts it on the kitchen table.* SANDRA *enters, pauses, and moves to hug* REA.

| | |
|---|---|
| **SANDRA** | Hello Rea. |
| **REA** | Sandra, I didn't realize I was late, I thought you said noon. |
| **SANDRA** | I did, Cerise just came over early. |
| **REA** | Oh? *(turns to get her bags)* |
| **SANDRA** | Assata, what did your Auntie Rea do to her hair? |
| **REA** | I haven't done anything to my hair. |
| **SANDRA** | It looks different from when I last saw you. |
| **REA** | It's the first time I've worn it out. |
| **ASSATA** | I think it looks good. |
| **DEHLIA** | *(yelling from the kitchen)* Sandy the water is boiling. |
| **SANDRA** | So. |

> *She starts to go towards the kitchen.*

| | |
|---|---|
| **DEHLIA** | So you not coming in to look at it. |

**CERISE**  *(gathering her grocery bags)* I better take this stuff in there.

**REA**  Sandra you didn't tell me to bring anything.

**SANDRA**  Oh I thought we could make the dumplings. But I see you brought stuff anyway.

**REA**  Just a few things, some yam, daschene, pumpkin, sea salt, garlic press....

**SANDRA**  Well, lets bring it in the kitchen. Assata, come show your Auntie Rea your—

**ASSATA**  I will in a minute Mom I just gotta finish something out here.

**SANDRA**  Probably the phone.

## Peeling, Chopping, Cutting        Scene Seven

SANDRA, CERISE, *and* REA *go into the kitchen.* DEHLIA *and* REA *smile politely at each other. Ancestral time,* ASSATA *stays in living room, playing with the mangoes.*

CERISE *enters the kitchen, dumps her groceries, and watches* DEHLIA *doing the puzzle. She tries to help but it's not her forte.* SANDRA *and* REA *start to unpack* REA's *bag on the kitchen table, crowding out* DEHLIA.

**DEHLIA**  *(to* REA*)* Rea, we already went grocery shopping this morning.

**REA**  I see Sandy does the cooking and you do the—

**DEHLIA**  Nice of you to come, Rea.

| | |
|---|---|
| **REA** | Thank you for inviting me. |
| **DEHLIA** | You'll have to thank your sister San— |
| **SANDRA** | She did. |

> *Pause.*

| | |
|---|---|
| **REA** | Well, I better start chopping up the provisions. |
| **SANDRA** | Yes we're all here now. *(pause)* Except for Assata. |
| **DEHLIA** | She'll be along. |

> CERISE *throws down a puzzle piece.*

| | |
|---|---|
| **CERISE** | Dehlia, what kind of puzzle is this? *(picks up puzzle-box cover)* Where's the picture? |
| **DEHLIA** | There is no picture. |
| **CERISE** | What do you mean no picture? That would drive me crazy. |
| **DEHLIA** | The fun is in doing it. Cerise maybe you need a hobby, one that doesn't involve lying down so much. |
| **CERISE** | What's the point in putting in all that hard work if you don't know how its going to turn out. |
| **SANDRA** | Just like the soup. |
| **CERISE** | Just like sex. |

> REA *starts washing the provisions.*

| | |
|---|---|
| **REA** | Depends on how long it takes. You taste it as you go along. |
| **CERISE** | How many have you tasted, Rea? |
| **REA** | Enough. I make *soup* quite often. |

| | |
|---|---|
| **DEHLIA** | You not putting any of that kuchi, kulchah stuff in the soup. |
| **SANDRA** | Kuchela. You leave us Trinis alone, don't you Jamaicans drink Irish Moss? |
| **CERISE** | Is that the thing you made for me Dehlia... with the seaweed? |
| **DEHLIA** | You said you wanted something to make it last. |
| **CERISE** | Make *him* last not me. |
| **SANDRA** | *(to* DEHLIA*)* What you know about cooking? |
| **DEHLIA** | Yeah, I know... I had Esta. |
| **SANDRA** | Rea, how did you find this stuff, its exactly what Mummy used to put in her soup. |
| **REA** | Well I wasn't even going to bring anything, since you didn't tell me everyone else was asked to bring something. |
| **SANDRA** | I want us to make the dumplings. |
| | REA *starts peeling, chopping, and cutting.* SANDRA *gets a knife and joins her. Spotlight up on* SANDRA *with knife in her hand. She's back in lecture mode. In ancestral time,* REA *continues chopping,* ASSATA *mango chowing, and* DEHLIA *and* CERISE *shuffle puzzle pieces.* |
| **SANDRA** | The middle passage... the surgical removal of female reproductive organs.... I received some interesting papers on this topic.... Women were kept at the bottom of the ship, as they fetched less of a price than a stud; a few were kept on-deck to cook for the captain, and some were used for.... You see, a good doctor will tell you as many facts as possible about the... give you books to read, but a brilliant historian... Indian women... |

anley as a Reaganite.

sse Jackson running for president.

itlins *a la flambe*.

els good.

o on.

n going to chop up the next teacher that questions I'm "cultivating an environment conducive to rning for my daughter."

ush them up—

with your Ph.D.

ndra you would never do that.

ne for things to change.

at's changing?

SANDRA) Let it out. This is the place.

at's what's changing.

ne people never change. My mom wanted me to a government job.

your mom hated her job.

, but "we don't have the luxuries they do, we have work twice as hard as—"

know, maybe your mother had a point, Cerise. nmaking—that's what you do isn't it?—is osed to be cutthroat.

ere is it you work again?

| | |
|---|---|
| **REA** | ...they can be your sistah... |
| **SANDRA** | ...single and widowed... whatever caste were... |

*REA, ASSATA, and DEHLIA speak together, but DEHLIA adds her on take on it.*

| | |
|---|---|
| **REA/ ASSATA** | ...they can be your sistah. |
| **DEHLIA** | ...they can be your sistah-in-*law*. |
| **SANDRA** | ...whatever caste were forced to cross the Kala Pani and become indentured labourers or face death... *(pause)* many faced death no matter what they did. |

*Spotlight comes down, and* SANDRA *continues chopping, peeling, and cutting.* CERISE *and* DEHLIA *put away the puzzle and start chopping.*

## Peeling, Chopping, Cutting      Scene Eight

*ASSATA takes the bowl, ingredients, and knife from their hiding place and sits on the floor, playing with the knife. This character has now moved into real time.*

*All four of them are around the kitchen table, doing peeling, chopping, and cutting motions;* DEHLIA *doing the plantain,* CERISE *doing the potatoes, and* REA *and* SANDRA *doing the provisions* REA *brought. Throughout this scene everyone gives their sounds of testifying.*

| | |
|---|---|
| **REA** | Chop it thin. |
| **SANDRA** | Don't chop it, slice it. |

ASSATA     *(in living room to herself)* I don't even want to be here.

DEHLIA     I can't peel the skin off of this.

ASSATA     *(in living room)* Cooking. A few years ago we were just fine. Cleaning. Now all of a sudden everything has to be just like it was in Trinidad. Cook with love.

SANDRA/
REA     If you can eat, you can cook.

ASSATA     *(in living room)* How about *buy* Mickey Dee's with love.

REA     Slowly, do it slowly, trust me it'll turn out better.

DEHLIA     We always do it slowly!

        *Sounds of laughter.*

ASSATA     We used to skin teeth, laugh.... *(sounds of laughter from the kitchen)* Well we're not in Trinidad. Chopping. We didn't have Dehlia in Trinidad. Seriousness. I'd go to New York over Trinidad any day.

REA     Do we have to talk about that?

ASSATA     Beat. Mom said "Lets go to New York." Just like that. For the day. Stir. We drive to Buffalo, take the first plane to New York, take a bus to downtown Manhattan, and by five p.m. we had bought like nuff stuff and we're sitting in a restaurant talking. Like big women y'know. Melt. Next morning, Mom and I are sitting around the kitchen table. Toast. Dehlia asks us "What's up?" Mom just smiles. Didn't say anything. It was like it was our little secret. Flavour.

---

AS
m
an
pu
to
sc

CERISE     I neve
betwe

SANDRA     Pare i
down

DEHLIA     Peel i
pull i
on. Ju
pee!

CERISE     I wan
gimm

REA     That

CERISE     Oh!

REA     I was
stree

DEHLIA     Whe

CERISE     Girl
cook

SANDRA     I wa

CERISE     Hmr

REA     Only

SANDRA     Eric

REA     Eigh
pati

DEHLIA

CERISE

DEHLIA

SANDRA

CERISE

REA

CERISE

DEHLIA

SANDRA

REA

CERISE

SANDRA

CERISE

DEHLIA

CERISE

REA

CERISE

| | |
|---|---|
| **REA** | I'm a senior policy advisor in the Ministry of Culture and Communications. |
| **CERISE** | The government. |
| **REA** | Yes. |
| **CERISE** | How do you stand it in there? |
| **REA** | Well, I try not to blow— |
| **CERISE** | Really, I don't mind it at all. |
| **REA** | Blow, you know lose my cool. Just yesterday, Mr. McDuff said *you* people are good at blah, blah, blahblahblahblahaaaaaaaaahblah.... |

> REA *continues under* SANDRA*'s yelling with a government droning sound, until her next line is heard.* CERISE *and* DEHLIA *make blah-blah sounds.*

| | |
|---|---|
| **SANDRA** | *(yelling)* Assata. Dehlia, what is that child doing in there? |
| **REA** | I told him that I didn't appreciate his comment and I would send a recommendation to... blah, blah, blahblahblahblahaaaaaaaaahblah.... |

> REA *continues under* SANDRA*'s yelling with a government droning sound, until her next line is heard.* CERISE *and* DEHLIA *make blah-blah sounds.*

| | |
|---|---|
| **SANDRA** | *(yelling)* Assata. *(to* DEHLIA*)* Isn't she going to help with this soup? |
| **REA** | I presented it last week. He hasn't looked at it yet, but I've filed a complaint with human res— blah, blah, blahblahblahblahaaaaaaaaahblah.... |

> REA *continues under* SANDRA*'s yelling with a*
> *government droning sound, until end of scene.*
> CERISE *and* DEHLIA *make blah-blah sounds.*

**SANDRA**      Why can't she try more?

**ASSATA**      *(takes a leftover mango, caresses it)* Mmmm a ripe
one... *(bites into it, then spits some out)* It's rotten.
How can it look fine on the outside and be....
*(smashes and pounds the mango with her fists)* Why
can't she try more?

> ASSATA *gets up and takes the bowl of Mango*
> *Chow into the kitchen.*

**DEHLIA**      She does. Maybe it's not always your way—

**SANDRA**      *(yelling to* ASSATA*)* Can't you hear me?

# Peeling, Chopping, Cutting     Scene Nine

> ASSATA *enters kitchen from living room.*

**ASSATA**      I'm right here, you don't have to ye—

**SANDRA**      Yell.

**CERISE**      *(to* ASSATA*)* So what are you up to?

**ASSATA**      I made Mom's favorite.

**SANDRA**      Really?

**DEHLIA**      You bettah than me.

**REA**      Good for you Assata.

**SANDRA**      I didn't see you by the pot.

| | |
|---|---|
| **ASSATA** | Its ready, I made it out there by myself. |
| | ASSATA *hands* SANDRA *the bowl of Mango Chow from behind her back.* SANDRA *is speechless.* |
| **DEHLIA** | *(feigning surprise)* What's that? Green mango chopped up? |
| **REA** | Is that Mango Chow? *(takes bowl from* SANDRA *and tries a piece)* It's good, its almost like back home. |
| **ASSATA** | I know. I got Granma's recipe. |
| **REA** | But honey, Granma died just before you left Trinidad, you were only two. |
| **ASSATA** | I mean my daddy's granma. |
| **SANDRA** | When did you talk to her? |
| **ASSATA** | I called her in Trinidad. *(to her mother)* I'll pay for it. |
| **REA** | Sandy, I didn't know you still talk to them. |
| **SANDRA** | I don't. Nothing happened. But since Tony died, I just lost touch. No time.... |
| **ASSATA** | Time. For. Things. To change. |
| **SANDRA** | Didn't I ask you to come help with the soup? |
| **ASSATA** | What's the difference, I made something. Besides, you said Mango Chow is your favorite. |
| **SANDRA** | But I wanted you to help with the soup, don't you have anything to add!! |
| **DEHLIA** | Sandy, she can still help. |
| **SANDRA** | I wanted her to be in here, chopping and ting with everyone else. |

**DEHLIA**     There's still time.

**SANDRA**     The water is boiling.

**REA**     That's the best time.

**SANDRA**     *(to* ASSATA*)* Don't cut your eye at me Assata, you know what you were supposed to do and you didn't do it. You would rather sit in the living room and chat on the phone than—

**ASSATA**     I wasn't on the phone, I was chopping the mango— forget it.

          ASSATA *storms into the living room and puts on her walkwoman.*

          *Pause.*

**CERISE**     Girl, when you let it out, you let it out hard.

          CERISE *exits to living room and watches* ASSATA.

          *Pause.*

**DEHLIA**     *(to* SANDRA*)* What are you really mad at Sandy?

          DEHLIA *follows* CERISE *to the living room and remains hidden, watching* CERISE *and* ASSATA. REA *is rooted to the spot, spotlight up, as* SANDRA *does her lecture.*

**SANDRA**     There has been a change in the syllabus, oral stories will not be allowed as a valid historical document. It's beyond my control.

          *Spotlight down.* SANDRA *is with* REA *in the kitchen.*

# Peeling, Chopping, Cutting        Scene Ten

> DEHLIA, CERISE, *and* ASSATA *in the living room, while* REA *continues chopping.*

**SANDRA**   Here let me help.

**REA**   Food doesn't taste right from an angry cook.

> SANDRA *sits down and* REA *continues chopping.*

**REA**   Wait until you simmer down.

> *Gradually* SANDRA *starts to rock back and forth in sync with* REA*'s chopping motion, in ancestral time.*

> ASSATA *is listening to her walkwoman.* CERISE *approaches* ASSATA.

**CERISE**   Your mom's probably had these up-and-down moods for awhile.

> ASSATA *doesn't acknowledge that she heard* CERISE, *but keeps listening to her music.*

**CERISE**   You heard me, I know you did.

**ASSATA**   *(doesn't take off the walkwoman)* Does she have to talk to me like that in front of everyone.

**CERISE**   Mothers talk, sometimes you just don't want to hear what they have to say.

**ASSATA**   Do *they* listen?

**CERISE**   Sometimes they don't want to hear what we have to say.

> DEHLIA *enters, takes the walkwoman from* ASSATA. ASSATA *glares at* DEHLIA *as* DEHLIA *puts the walkwoman on and starts to dance. Both* CERISE *and* ASSATA *start laughing.* DEHLIA *stops and puts down walkwoman.* ASSATA *grabs it but doesn't put it on; she fiddles with it.*

**ASSATA**   I made her favourite thing... from Trinidad.

**CERISE**   *(to* ASSATA*)* She knows.

**DEHLIA**   She wants the soup.

**ASSATA**   I don't. I want things the way they were.

**DEHLIA**   We all do. I need to remember the first time I met the two of you. It was cold and you were all bundled up in this pink snowsuit.

**CERISE**   And let me guess, she was this big.

> CERISE *gestures how small* ASSATA *must have been, exaggerating.*

**ASSATA**   I was ten. I was this big. *(shows them)*

**DEHLIA**   You know this country is cold. Esta warned me... Esta gave me a sweater somebody had sent her from foreign.

**ASSATA**   ...a sweater.

**CERISE**   *(to* DEHLIA*)* Who is taking the drugs you or Sandra?

**DEHLIA**   Neither of us. Sandra stopped chemo last year.

**CERISE**   I didn't know.

**ASSATA**   I knew it.

**DEHLIA**    She is trying other things, Assata.

**ASSATA**    Like what?

**DEHLIA**    Eating good food.

**ASSATA**    Like that will cure her.

**CERISE**    *(to* ASSATA*)* You can try to stop it from eating at you.

**ASSATA**    How?

**CERISE**    My mom never even tried.

**DEHLIA**    Your mom took everything they gave her.

**CERISE**    Yeah, everything... the shit they dished out, the long hours with little pay....

**ASSATA**    That's not her fault.

**DEHLIA**    Sandy lets things eat at her.

**ASSATA**    Am I eating at her?

> *Ancestral time.* CERISE *and* DEHLIA *comfort* ASSATA *in silence, rocking back and forth.* SANDRA *and* REA *are rocking in the kitchen.*

## Boiling!            Scene Eleven

          CERISE, DEHLIA, *and* ASSATA *in the living room.*

**CERISE**     *(quietly)* It's serious.

          ASSATA *goes into the kitchen.* DEHLIA *and* CERISE *follow to find* SANDRA *moving in sync with* REA, *who is continuing the chopping motion.* SANDRA *turns to see* ASSATA. ASSATA *picks up the plate of chopped provisions—the edoe, daschene, etc—to put some in the soup. No plantain or dumplings are added at this time.*

          SANDRA *helps* ASSATA. *She takes some provisions and drops them in the soup, and then stirs it.*

**SANDRA**     Old and....

          ASSATA *puts some spice in the soup.*

**ASSATA**     New.

          *On each of their lines,* DEHLIA, REA, *and* CERISE *also drop the chopped vegetables into the soup. They are all around the pot, making stirring motions.*

          DEHLIA *takes some provisions and drops them into the pot.*

**DEHLIA**     Me and you.

          REA *takes some provisions and drops them into the pot.*

REA           Kuchala with....

ASSATA        Kool-aid made from....

              CERISE *takes some provisions and drops them into the pot.*

CERISE        Kool-aid?

ASSATA        Kool-aid in mango flavour.

SANDRA        Why not?

REA           Free enterprise.

SANDRA        Recipe of the century.

REA           An historical lime.

ASSATA        With the essence of time.

CERISE        T-I-M-E.

DEHLIA        T-H-Y-M-E.

SANDRA        Tarragon. *(starts to add some to the soup)*

REA           And... curry powder. *(adds some to the soup)*

ASSATA        Ground up fine.

DEHLIA        Like sands in an hour glass.

SANDRA        When you cut a cucumber, *(she demonstrates)* slice the ends off and then take those pieces and rub each end of the cucumber. This takes the bitterness from it.

REA           If I rub my sistah, from her head to her toes will that take away the bitterness from her?

DEHLIA        Is it an English cucumber or a hybrid?

> *Pause.*

**REA**      A hybrid.

**SANDRA**      What about the plantain?

**DEHLIA**      Put it in later or it'll get soft 'n' mushy.

**CERISE**      It don't feel right in your mouth when it's soft 'n' mushy.

**SANDRA**      *(to CERISE)* Whatchya know about plantain? *(to DEHLIA)* Molly recipe that.

**DEHLIA**      Esta.

> *Spotlight on SANDRA as she does her lecture. DEHLIA, ASSATA, REA, and CERISE continue stirring the soup in ancestral time.*

**SANDRA**      When I say family, I mean it in the biggest sense. A complex, extended, non-traditional family, with its own secret language, a recipe to survive genocide. Nourish the good cells. Prepare the baby cell.

> *Spotlight comes down. SANDRA continues stirring the soup.*

**SANDRA**      *(to ASSATA)* I hope you're writing this recipe down.

> *REA moves towards the table, starts wiping it down, mumbles under her breath:*

**REA**      Plantain in soup?

> *DEHLIA moves towards table, joins REA, and "helps" wipe it down.*

**DEHLIA**      You start relaxing your hair now?

**REA**      We went through this in the living room. *No.*

CERISE    I've permed my hair at one time or the other. *(swings her hair to and fro)*

SANDRA    Cerise, do you have to play with your hair over the soup, you can tell you ain't Wes' Indian.

          SANDRA *shoos* CERISE *in the direction of the table, where she sits and watches* REA *and* DEHLIA *clean around her.* SANDRA *and* ASSATA *continue stirring the soup.*

CERISE    My hair is clean, I just got the braids put in.

DEHLIA    We had to take off our school hats when we were inside the house. Mama nevah let us wear them inside.

REA       Dehlia, we're not talking about "hats" the topics are soup and hair.

SANDRA    It all makes sense in Dehlia's mind. *(tastes the soup)* Rea, pass the salt.

CERISE    Sexual positions are the only things in Dehlia's mind.

ASSATA    *(to* CERISE*)* I don't want to think about it!

CERISE    Think about what...?

REA       Oh you mean your mother and Dehlia!

ASSATA    *Yes!* No! I mean *parents* having sex!

CERISE    Why? They make noise?

DEHLIA    Sunday afternoon, Esta had gone to country. Me, Mommy, and Daddy sat down on the verandah, with three bowls of grapenut ice-cream, no I lie, Daddy had rum 'n' raisin, him always like him rum. Anyway, we laugh till we drop.

CERISE    So?

| | |
|---|---|
| **DEHLIA** | That's how I found out! |
| | *Pause.* |
| **CERISE** | How did I find out? |
| **ASSATA** | When will I find out? |
| **REA** | Not now. |
| **SANDRA** | *(to* ASSATA*)* Well honey, at least you and I had a talk, our mommy *(indicates to* REA*)* never told us anything, I had to learn with your father. |
| **REA** | Don't tell a lie Sandy. |
| **SANDRA** | We never had sex. |
| **DEHLIA** | Who? |
| **REA** | So what did you do up on Maracas beach whole night? |
| **SANDRA** | Talk. |
| **ASSATA** | That's what I told you, Mom, when I— |
| **DEHLIA** | Who? |
| **REA** | Octopus. |
| **DEHLIA** | Octopus? |
| **SANDRA** | Reggie Alleyne... he was... |
| **REA** | A Belmont boy.... |
| **SANDRA** | ...he was going to teach me how to drive standard, so we went up to.... |
| **CERISE** | So what did he use as the stick shift? |
| **REA** | Exactly. |

SANDRA He drove. We parked. He put my hand on the stick shift...

CERISE ...it was bigger than you thought...

SANDRA ...I put it in reverse and walked home.

REA I wish you'd told me.

DEHLIA Kissing is sex.

ASSATA Well then, I've had sex.

REA What?

ASSATA Well Dehlia said—

SANDRA You *are* talking about kissing, not sex.

DEHLIA It depends on what kind of kissing.

CERISE I never allow the "tongue" in on the first date.

REA I don't like it at all.

DEHLIA Poor James.

CERISE *(to* REA*)* Girl, you don't know what you're missing. If they have a nice size tongue and know how to work it... hmmh... hmmh... hmmh!

REA No.... *(she mumbles)*

CERISE Why?

REA He has a rough tongue.

CERISE Oh! That must hurt when he goes.... *(gestures downwards)*

ASSATA That's rude. *(looks towards her mom for approval)*

| | |
|---|---|
| **SANDRA** | Assata, come help me with the soup.... *(mumbles as she moves towards the pot)* |
| **ASSATA** | *(whispers to* CERISE*)* So anyway, if the tongue is— |
| **REA** | Look, go help your mother.... *(to* CERISE*)* So. You mean the tongue should be smooth— |
| **DEHLIA** | *(interrupts)* No. A rough tongue can feel good, it just has to.... |
| **REA** | How do you know.... *(realizes, looking at* SANDRA*)* OH! You need help, Sandra? |

> REA *gets up and rushes towards* SANDRA *and* ASSATA *by the stove.* CERISE *winks at* DEHLIA, *who is bringing out her puzzle.* CERISE *groans but starts doing it anyways.* REA, SANDRA, *and* ASSATA *are stirring the soup.*

# Boiling!                                   Scene Twelve

| | |
|---|---|
| **SANDRA** | *(to* REA*)* So how is James? |
| **REA** | Well if you had invited him... because it's family isn't it? |
| **SANDRA** | *You and I* are what I wanted to deal with. |

> SANDRA *gives the stirring spoon to* ASSATA, *and moves to dust off the kitchen table. Satisfied, she moves to get broom to sweep the kitchen.*

| | |
|---|---|
| **DEHLIA** | You know my family didn't get invited either Rea! |

**CERISE**   Well I'm glad they're not coming... *(gets up from doing puzzle and ends up doing nothing)* ...not enough room *(looking around)* or soup for *both* sides of the family.

**ASSATA**   Natalie didn't get to come, and she's my best friend.

**REA**   They.... they are not family.

**SANDRA**   It's *my* definition of family.

**ASSATA**   *(stirring soup)* Uh... uh... soup's heating up.

**REA**   And that's that. Right Sandra?

**DEHLIA**   *(to ASSATA)* Put the peppah in.

**SANDRA**   Wait!

**ASSATA**   What? *(stops)*

**REA**   *(thinking SANDRA means her)* I said, you always have the last word.

> SANDRA *puts the broom down, rinses her hands, and moves towards the stove to check the soup.*

**SANDRA**   Rea. I was talking to Assata, I don't want the peppah in yet. *(stirs the soup)* It smells good, just a bit more....

**ASSATA**   Pepper

**SANDRA**   Yes.

> ASSATA *puts in some bonnet pepper.*

**REA**   I just want to know why some people were invited and—

**SANDRA**   MY HOUSE.

**DEHLIA**     Our house... *(looks at* SANDRA*)* ...hon.

**REA**     Anyway Sandra I'm glad to be here, I just think that it's really important that you surround yourself with people, like, well like James and myself.

**SANDRA**     I think it's important that I have the people I want around me.

**REA**     Well, Assata's future is... and she is *my* niece.

**DEHLIA**     Assata's future is right here with me... and her mother.

**CERISE**     ...and me....

**SANDRA**     Her future is exactly why we're here.

**ASSATA**     What? What are you talking about?

**REA**     I'm pleased that it's finally out in the open.

**DEHLIA**     We're doing fine.

**CERISE**     Let's hear what Sandra has to say.

**REA**     *(looks at* CERISE*)* Do you think this is the time and place to discuss it Sandy?

**SANDRA**     This is exactly the time and the place. I need to know what everyone here can and will do to support Assata *and* Dehlia....

**ASSATA**     Are you giving up?

**REA**     The last time we talked Sandy, I thought you were trying alternative methods, now it seems you're not trying anything. One of James' clients is an onco-logist. I can get the number so you can call. But I also think we should prepare for the worst. *(pause)* You know... the insurance... a college fund for the child. James' daddy has invited us to come home and we'd like to take Assata to Trinidad.

**SANDRA**   So Dehlia, you going Trinidad?

**DEHLIA**   Auntie Dotilda and dem have a sixteen-year-old boy child.

**REA**   So?

**DEHLIA**   So she... Assata won't be alone when we all go down next summer.

**SANDRA**   It's not confirmed yet Dehlia. I am not talking just about summer, I'm talking about what we all can do together....

**REA**   I want Assata to be raised like I was in a proper Trini home.

**SANDRA**   So, if Dehlia was a Trini it would be okay?

**DEHLIA**   Most of the raising has been done. By me... *(she takes her time)* ...and Sandra.

**SANDRA**   Rea, pass the salt.

**REA**   No, I'll do it... your hand was always too heavy.

**SANDRA**   Do it with love.

REA *sucks her teeth, puts down the salt.*

**ASSATA**   Is anyone interested in what I think?

**CERISE**   I'm listening.

**REA**   I'm her family... what if anything... was to ever happen.

**DEHLIA**   Nothing is going to happen.

## Boiling! Scene Thirteen

ASSATA *moves to go into the living room.*

**SANDRA**  Where are you going?

*Dehlia pulls her back down in the chair.*

**DEHLIA**  Relax Sandy.

**SANDRA**  I just want her here, she's always running.

ASSATA *reluctantly stays.*

**DEHLIA**  Maybe she needs time-out.

**REA**  I think Sandy knows her own child.

**DEHLIA**  Rea, for the last time she is our child.

**CERISE**  Is anyone listening to Assata?

**REA**  What's the matter you worried she might turn out too Indian, she might like men.

**DEHLIA**  Why don't you and your man go have a child?

**SANDRA**  That is not the point.

**REA**  We can't.

**SANDRA**  I want the soup to be like it was back home. Dumplings—cornmeal and flour—no plantain, ground provisions, no mango. Taste exactly like back home. A real Wes' Indian family. No fighting.

**REA**  We fought.

| | |
|---|---|
| **CERISE** | I'm not West Indian, I don't know the ground rules. |
| **DEHLIA** | We're here now. We are a Wes' Indian family. It's going to taste like us. |
| **CERISE** | I do know how to support Assata and Dehlia. |
| **REA** | What about me? I'm *the* family. |
| **SANDRA** | This is my family. |
| **REA** | Sandy, I don't know why you carrying on? This isn't like any soup I know back home. |
| **SANDRA** | But it could be Rea, we have all the same ingredients. |
| **REA** | No, we don't. Things change. The food doesn't even come from the same place. You've romanticized this back home, back home. What hasn't changed is the way a child should be brought up—with James and I. |
| **SANDRA** | We were raised by one woman. |
| **DEHLIA** | Yes, Rea things change. Families change. |
| **REA** | You and Dehlia... it's a lot to handle. |
| **SANDRA** | You couldn't make an effort to get along this one time? A lot to handle? I wanted a dinner, one dinner with the people that I care about. Try waking up each morning, deciding whether or not to be drugged up, or sit with the pain all day. Getting needles stuck in you. It took me three hours to get off the bed this morning. A lot to handle? Fuckery! Pure fuckery running through my blood. |

ASSATA *moves beside* SANDRA.

| | |
|---|---|
| **ASSATA** | Am I a lot to handle? |

SANDRA *turns and slaps* ASSATA.

| | |
|---|---|
| **SANDRA** | This not about you! |

> ASSATA *is stunned and runs into the living
> room.* CERISE *follows, and calls after her.*

**CERISE**     Baby, are you all right?

**DEHLIA**     Sandy! You caan rule everybody. It's one thing the
way you treat me and everyone else, but Assata. You
want to stop surgery okay, you want to stop chemo,
you want some Trini diet, okay. You want your sister
okay. But Assata. NO!

> DEHLIA *storms out into the living room.*
> CERISE *and* DEHLIA *comfort* ASSATA.
> SANDRA*'s in the kitchen, crying and holding
> herself, while* REA *sits in silence.*

> *Silence.*

**SANDRA**     I lost my temper. I lost control. Casualties. I lost
control of the situation.... I've LOST! This war.
Fighting, and trying to control my child. I've hit her.
Fighting. This gift from my womb, and... this thing
in my womb. I have done something terrible. My
daughter. Where do you have time to learn. *(a piece of
pain hits SANDRA in the womb; she looks down
and sees blood running between her legs)* Blood.

> REA *comes and helps her change her skirt.
> Ashamed,* SANDRA *unwraps her skirt and hides
> the bloodstained wrap in the corner.* SANDRA
> *now sits with her hand rubbing her belly, almost
> like she's pregnant.* REA *comforts* SANDRA.
> CERISE, DEHLIA. *and* ASSATA *are in the
> living room.*

# Simmering                                    Scene Fourteen

*Convergence of ancestral and real time.*
*SANDRA and REA get up and go to the kitchen*
*table, and start to prepare the dumplings,*
*measuring the flour, salt, cornmeal, and water,*
*mixing it in a large, beige, ceramic bowl,*
*making these repeated motions/movements*
*together.*

**REA**          A Long Time

**SANDRA**       A Lifetime.

**REA**          Yes.

REA *starts looking for a board to roll out the*
*dumplings on.* SANDRA *takes out a battered,*
*wooden bread board and hands it to* REA.

**SANDRA**       Use this.

REA *holds it in astonishment and presses it*
*towards herself.*

**REA**          How?

**SANDRA**       It arrived just in time.

**REA**          It was my daddy's. Mine.

**SANDRA**       All yours Re. Not my daddy.

**REA**          I'm Indian.

**SANDRA**       Half Re—

**REA**          My daddy is a whole man, was a whole man.

| | |
|---|---|
| **SANDRA** | Our mama was a whole woman. |
| **REA** | All black and... all Indian |
| **SANDRA** | History in the flesh. |
| **REA** | A mutation? |
| **SANDRA** | Variation. |
| **REA** | Unique. |
| **SANDRA** | Ten percent of the population is...? |

*Pause.*

| | |
|---|---|
| **REA** | Dogla. Half black half Indian.... |
| **SANDRA** | Gay. *(pause)* A mutation? |
| **REA** | No. A variation. |

*They both return to rolling out the dumplings.*

# Simmering                           Scene Fifteen

ASSATA, DEHLIA, *and* CERISE *in the living room.*

| | |
|---|---|
| **CERISE** | My mother died of cancer. |
| **ASSATA** | What kind? |
| **CERISE** | Not in her womb. |
| **ASSATA** | Breast? |

CERISE   It ate away both her breasts and started to feed on....
         She died a bag of bones, screaming at me.

ASSATA   My mom was just screaming.

CERISE   I know. Your mom needs to scream, my mom needed
         to listen.

ASSATA   Why?

CERISE   Your mom never lets it out.

ASSATA   I mean why did your mom need to listen?

CERISE   I don't want to have cancer. I don't want to be like
         my mother. She was miserable.

ASSATA   What made her miserable?

CERISE   Until today, I thought it was me.

ASSATA   What was it?

CERISE   Nothing and Everything, her supervisor, the loans
         officer... and nothing.

ASSATA   What?

CERISE   My mother never saw the joy in anything, nothing
         was ever right.

         SANDRA *and* REA *finish the dumplings.*
         SANDRA *sends* REA *out.*

SANDRA   Go call Assata. *(puts the dumplings in the soup, then
         decides to put the plantain in the soup)* Plantain.

         REA *enters the living room and watches from
         the back. Ancestral time. Lights dim on*
         SANDRA *as she grabs her womb and does a
         rocking motion, maybe humming, crying sounds
         come from her.*

**CERISE**     Years later, just after we found out she had cancer, her and me and my aunt were sitting around talking about my cousin being a boy child and my aunt having to do "The Talk." My mom offered that there were lots of good books nowadays. Again. Fuck. In front of me. Talking about a book! She's seen more shit than I can even imagine.... I wonder, if we never went through slavery if we would still have all this shit.

**ASSATA**     I wonder...

                REA *moves closer.*

**REA**       ...if we never went through slavery...

**DEHLIA**    ...if she would have this shit.

                ASSATA *moves into* CERISE*'s arms, and they rock.*

**ASSATA**     It's alright Cerise.

**REA**       *(to* CERISE*)* It seems *we* all share similar stories.

**DEHLIA**    When I used to get headache, my mom would tell me to stop thinking about boys.

**CERISE**     *(to* DEHLIA*)* Everytime you can't deal with something you go and space out.

**DEHLIA**    I used to get a headache when "Granma from Redhill came to visit."

**ASSATA**     "Granma from Redhill"?

**REA**       We used to call it the "curse."

**ASSATA**     We call it my "thing" at school, but Mom says she's "flowing."

**CERISE**     I like that "flooowing."

ASSATA      My mom still rubs my belly with almond oil and
            tells me to let it out. So we....

DEHLIA      They groan together.

ASSATA      You love it Dehlia, you're right in there too.

DEHLIA      Yeah but my groan is melodic.

REA         Our mother used to do that for us.

ASSATA      Your groan is....

            *ASSATA starts to let out a groan,* DEHLIA
            *starts to riff on it.*

REA         No, no you're supposed to do it from your diaphram.

            *She demonstrates.*

ASSATA      Any sound will do. C'mon Auntie Cerise.

            CERISE *starts to let out a low growl.*

DEHLIA      It's not sex Cerise, it's womb pain.

REA         Sometimes it's the same thing.

            CERISE *continues with her growl.* ASSATA
            *joins her,* DEHLIA *follows, and finally* REA.
            *They all start to do a soundscape of womb pain
            that continues under* SANDRA*'s rocking
            movement.*

REA         *(to* ASSATA*)* Your mom wants to see you.

## Boiling!                                    Scene Sixteen

ASSATA *goes into the kitchen.* CERISE,
DEHLIA, *and* REA *sit in the living room,*
*continuing their soundscape.*

**ASSATA**      What?

*Silence.*

**SANDRA**      I'm sorry, I had no right to.... I know I shouldn't
have hit you. Nobody deserves to be hit. I'm old
enough and big enough to rationalize my feelings.

**ASSATA**      Don't.

**SANDRA**      Assa....

**ASSATA**      No.

**SANDRA**      Do you know how hard I have worked to....

**ASSATA**      Why?

**SANDRA**      I... I lost control.

**ASSATA**      Control? What do you think I am...? Some pet?

**SANDRA**      I'm tired.

**ASSATA**      I don't care.

**SANDRA**      I'm your mother and you—

**ASSATA**      No. You listen to me now. I'm not you. I hate you.
You're ugly.

**SANDRA**    You are such a selfish, self-centred.... You always turn it back to yourself.

**ASSATA**    No. You hate that you won't be here to shape me, mold me, pick on me. Well you know what, Mom? Dehlia, Cerise, Auntie Re, and I will be just fine.

**SANDRA**    You want me to die?

**ASSATA**    Umm.... Mom, I'm not saying I want you to die, but you treat me like a fool.

**SANDRA**    There are things you learn as you get older....

**ASSATA**    You never let me talk. All you want to talk about is what you want. You walk away whenever I talk to you. You shut me up when I talk about my.... You never stop lecturing. You stop... me.

**SANDRA**    I told you I made a mistake, one mistake can be forgiven.

**ASSATA**    What about my mistakes? You never forget. You don't trust me. Always on me, about my friends.

**SANDRA**    I just want to spend time with you.

**ASSATA**    Well that's what I want Mom... more time.

**SANDRA**    Me too.

**ASSATA**    You've been mean, you haven't liked me, the one that's not you, but a part of you. Am I going to get sick? Is this how it's going to be for me? How come everyone close to me in my life has died? My granma, my father, and.... I'm eating at you. It's me, isn't it.... I'm scared. I....

**SANDRA**    Cancer. Some parasite feeding on my womb. The nerve.

**ASSATA**    Uncontrollable.

| | |
|---|---|
| **SANDRA** | Invisible. |
| **ASSATA** | Blood? |
| **SANDRA** | Maybe. |
| **ASSATA** | When? |
| **SANDRA** | Soon. |
| **ASSATA** | Why? |
| **SANDRA** | It's time... it's time to serve the Mango Chow. |
| **ASSATA** | Why are you giving up? |
| **SANDRA** | I'm not Assata. I'm fighting with everything I have left. Cutting and more cutting until there is nothing left of my womb. Three years of cutting and slicing, and pricking and burning. Cursing myself each day for not being more careful. It didn't feel like *my* body anymore. So many things in my life have been beyond my control. I'm doing the... cutting, chopping, and slicing. With help from my daughter. |

> *Pause.*

| | |
|---|---|
| **ASSATA** | I want you to rub my belly, who will? I wish you didn't have to feel pain. I wish.... |
| **SANDRA** | You need to make peace... peace with me Assata. |
| **ASSATA** | I'm not at war with you. You need to make peace with yourself. |
| **SANDRA** | Something burning? |
| **ASSATA** | Only candles. |

> DEHLIA *enters the kitchen with a candle. She sets it down.* CERISE *and* REA *stay in the living room.*

*Silence.*

**REA**        I hope they'll be okay.

**DEHLIA**     You okay hon?

**CERISE**     They will.

> CERISE *puts some soul music on the boom box.* CERISE *and* REA *light candles and incense.*

**ASSATA**     Yeah.

**SANDRA**     Mmmmh.

**DEHLIA**     Mmmmmh.

> CERISE *and* REA *enter kitchen with candles and incense, and set them down.*


# Dishing                          Scene Seventeen

**SANDRA**     Dehlia bring down those bowls.

> DEHLIA *gestures for* CERISE *to get them and rubs* SANDRA*'s back.* CERISE *goes to get the small soup bowls and* REA *stirs the soup.*

**DEHLIA**     Cerise, West Indian soup.

**CERISE**     Uhuh.

**DEHLIA**     Big bowls.

> CERISE *brings down five huge bowls for the soup.*

**ASSATA**    I'll get the spoons.

**CERISE**    I guess they're big too.

**REA**    We have big appetites, it takes a lot to feed us.

**SANDRA**    Are you hungry?

**REA**    Yes.

**CERISE**    Uhuh.

**DEHLIA**    Always.

> SANDRA *gets up and starts to dish out the soup.* CERISE *rushes up with her bowl, then* ASSATA, DEHLIA, *and* REA. *They all sit down at the table and eat their soup.*

# Nyamming                              Scene Eighteen

**REA**    Plantain in soup, taste good.

**DEHLIA**    Thank you.

**CERISE**    Which one is the plantain?

**ASSATA**    It looks like the banana.

**SANDRA**    It taste good. Sweet.

**CERISE**    The dumplings taste sweet too.

**REA**    I made them the Bajan way, I put some sugar in them.

**DEHLIA**    Sugar in dumplings? We put sugar in stew-chicken, sugar in—

| | |
|---|---|
| **SANDRA** | But that's not how we made them back home. |
| **REA** | Things change. |
| **CERISE** | I like them. |
| **SANDRA** | Me too. |

ASSATA *eats some soup, makes a face.*

| | |
|---|---|
| **ASSATA** | Ugh... daschene. |
| **REA** | That face reminds me of your mother's when she had to eat daschene. |
| **ASSATA** | Mom hates it too? |
| **REA** | Yes, and with our mother you never had a choice. *(imitating an older mother)* "I walked barefoot to school, food is scarce, money doesn't grow on trees...." |
| **ASSATA** | *(to REA)* It runs in the family, right Mom? |
| **SANDRA** | It's a good thing I used to give you my daschene. Maga skinny but could eat, and *(to the others)* would eat anything. |
| **REA** | Still do. |
| **DEHLIA** | My mother would take me to the hospice by Half-Way Tree and we would give out money to the old women who were left there. We couldn't tell Daddy. She didn't take Neville or Janice. |
| **REA** | Sandy, remember I got nuff buffs from Tony for being skinny. "You nah know woman supposed to be fat and nice like me wife Sandy?" |
| **ASSATA** | So my daddy liked his women plump. |
| **CERISE** | *(to ASSATA)* How do your men like you? |

| | |
|---|---|
| **ASSATA** | Most men are cads. |
| **SANDRA** | What would you know? |
| **ASSATA** | They rub up on you, crank down your neck while you busting a slow song, they can't sing and they have stinky breath. |
| **CERISE** | Some things never change. Remember "These Eyes the Place to Socialize"? |
| **SANDRA** | Oh gawd yes, we went there Rea. |
| **REA** | Oh yes. It had that flocked-velvet wall paper, disco globe in the ceiling, and you're praying, hoping that no man with drip-drip head is going to ask you to dance. |
| **CERISE** | I had to do this whole espionage business, just to get out. I was in a party. My mother, with her housecoat underneath her trench coat, came inside looking for me. My mother didn't have a loud voice. But I could hear her softly calling, "Cerise? Do you know Cerise? Have you seen Cerise?" I ran out that back door so fast. |
| **ASSATA** | I wouldn't know nothing about that. |
| **SANDRA** | You bettah not. |
| **CERISE** | When I got home my uncle beat me so hard I couldn't even think about party or boys. |
| **SANDRA** | Respect! Respect! |
| **REA** | Respect. It wasn't Aretha who taught me how to spell that, it was our mother. |
| **DEHLIA** | "R-E-S-P-E-C-T, that is what love means to me." What does the song say again? |
| **SANDRA** | Is it "love"? That doesn't even sound right. |

| | |
|---|---|
| **CERISE** | *(singing)* "Sock it to me, sock it to me, sock it to me." |
| **DEHLIA** | You would remember that part. |
| **ASSATA** | "Sock it to me"! I can't believe the stuff you all put in your music. |
| **REA** | What's in you music? |
| **ASSATA** | Deep stuff. |

> SANDRA *starts making fun of rapping,* DEHLIA *joins, then* CERISE, *and then* REA.

| | |
|---|---|
| **REA** | I knew that. |
| **ASSATA** | When did this big pot of water, spices, and stuff start to taste like soup. |
| **DEHLIA** | It's alchemy. |
| **REA** | It's magic. |
| **DEHLIA** | Alchemy is magic. |
| **CERISE** | It's Voodoo. |
| **ASSATA** | It's Obeah. |
| **SANDRA** | Sistahs. |
| **DEHLIA** | It's soup. |

> SANDRA *doubles over in pain. Lights come down onstage.*

**REA**          ...they can be your sistah...

**SANDRA**       ...single and widowed... whatever caste were...

                 REA, ASSATA, *and* DEHLIA *speak together,*
                 *but* DEHLIA *adds her on take on it.*

**REA/**
**ASSATA**       ...they can be your sistah.

**DEHLIA**       ...they can be your sistah-in-*law.*

**SANDRA**       ...whatever caste were forced to cross the Kala Pani
                 and become indentured labourers or face death...
                 *(pause)* many faced death no matter what they did.

                 *Spotlight comes down, and* SANDRA *continues*
                 *chopping, peeling, and cutting.* CERISE *and*
                 DEHLIA *put away the puzzle and start chopping.*

## Peeling, Chopping, Cutting          Scene Eight

                 ASSATA *takes the bowl, ingredients, and knife*
                 *from their hiding place and sits on the floor,*
                 *playing with the knife. This character has now*
                 *moved into real time.*

                 *All four of them are around the kitchen table,*
                 *doing peeling, chopping, and cutting motions;*
                 DEHLIA *doing the plantain,* CERISE *doing the*
                 *potatoes, and* REA *and* SANDRA *doing the*
                 *provisions* REA *brought. Throughout this scene*
                 *everyone gives their sounds of testifying.*

**REA**          Chop it thin.

**SANDRA**       Don't chop it, slice it.

ASSATA      *(in living room to herself)* I don't even want to be here.

DEHLIA      I can't peel the skin off of this.

ASSATA      *(in living room)* Cooking. A few years ago we were just fine. Cleaning. Now all of a sudden everything has to be just like it was in Trinidad. Cook with love.

SANDRA/
REA      If you can eat, you can cook.

ASSATA      *(in living room)* How about *buy* Mickey Dee's with love.

REA      Slowly, do it slowly, trust me it'll turn out better.

DEHLIA      We always do it slowly!

     *Sounds of laughter.*

ASSATA      We used to skin teeth, laugh.... *(sounds of laughter from the kitchen)* Well we're not in Trinidad. Chopping. We didn't have Dehlia in Trinidad. Seriousness. I'd go to New York over Trinidad any day.

REA      Do we have to talk about that?

ASSATA      Beat. Mom said "Lets go to New York." Just like that. For the day. Stir. We drive to Buffalo, take the first plane to New York, take a bus to downtown Manhattan, and by five p.m. we had bought like nuff stuff and we're sitting in a restaurant talking. Like big women y'know. Melt. Next morning, Mom and I are sitting around the kitchen table. Toast. Dehlia asks us "What's up?" Mom just smiles. Didn't say anything. It was like it was our little secret. Flavour.

ASSATA *starts peeling, cutting, and slicing the*
*mangoes, adds the pepper, vinegar, salt, lime,*
*and pepper sauce to the bowl of sliced mangoes,*
*puts the bowl aside, and covers it with a tea*
*towel. This action takes place throughout the*
*scene.*

CERISE    I never understood in cookbooks, the difference
          between pare and peel.

SANDRA    Pare is when someone from the department cuts you
          down in a faculty meeting, and peel is when—

DEHLIA    Peel is when I tear the skin off the bus drivers that
          pull into the station, park the bus, and won't let us
          on. Jus' mek us stand up in the cold while he goes
          pee!

CERISE    I wanna crush those guys who yell out "Sweetie,
          gimme your number."

REA       That never happens to me.

CERISE    Oh! Your pussy's too pricey.

REA       I was  spit on by this crazy old white man on my
          street.

DEHLIA    Where did it get you?

CERISE    Girl we in it now. We're cutting them up. Did you
          cook a lot back home?

SANDRA    I was too busy stirring up revolution.

CERISE    Hmmh. Black Power.

REA       Only no revolution took place.

SANDRA    Eric Williams as Prime Minister and no revolution.

REA       Eighties brought us oil and blue notes and French
          patisseries on a Caribbean mountaintop.

**DEHLIA**      Manley as a Reaganite.

**CERISE**      Jesse Jackson running for president.

**DEHLIA**      Chitlins *a la flambe*.

**SANDRA**      Feels good.

**CERISE**      Go on.

**SANDRA**      I'm going to chop up the next teacher that questions if I'm "cultivating an environment conducive to learning for my daughter."

**REA**        Mash them up—

**CERISE**      —with your Ph.D.

**DEHLIA**      Sandra you would never do that.

**SANDRA**      Time for things to change.

**REA**        What's changing?

**CERISE**      *(to* SANDRA*)* Let it out. This is the place.

**SANDRA**      That's what's changing.

**CERISE**      Some people never change. My mom wanted me to get a government job.

**DEHLIA**      But your mom hated her job.

**CERISE**      Yes, but "we don't have the luxuries they do, we have to work twice as hard as—"

**REA**        You know, maybe your mother had a point, Cerise. Filmmaking—that's what you do isn't it?—is supposed to be cutthroat.

**CERISE**      Where is it you work again?